A Vision Unseen
Colorblind Captures

Decades of being around accomplished artists producing absolutely phenomenal quality work has taught that we are capable of greatness. It is possible to meet our destiny and become it. Experiencing excellence done with such apparent magical ease and humble selfless gratification is the inspiration for this book of original photography.

Being colorblind gives an advantage when composing black & white... less confusion. The photos in this collection were selected from thousands of captures. All images were framed in the camera and presented without edits, genuine as seen through the lens. RAW conversion applied by proprietary panchromatic process.

Fine art prints available from original files.

info@ BEACHNOISE.com

- Joseph Fleming

0351

0345

0437

0464

0503

0531

0667

0705

0780

0826

0843

0920

0938

0975

1085

1088

1784

2042

2083

2180

2374

2397

2467

2495

2631

2929

2969

3147

3346

3359

3656

3720

3752

3916

3943

4035

4070

4099

4193

4265

4533

4879

5492

5541

5705

5750

5784

5811

5844

5846

5992

6014

6095

6176

6946

7148

7182

7339

7656

7693

7783

7939

8173

8345

8470

8471

8766

8889

8896

9024

9258

9292

9346

9353

9430

9970

9975

9980

9981

9992

PROFESSIONAL PORTFOLIO ONLINE

BeachNoise.com

Joseph Fleming

www.ingramcontent.com/pod-product-compliance
Lightning Source LLC
Chambersburg PA
CBHW040813200526

45159CB00022B/653